BETTER CROSS-COUNTRY RUNNING

for Boys and Girls

George Sullivan

Illustrated with photographs

DODD, MEAD & COMPANY · NEW YORK

PICTURE CREDITS

All photographs are by George Sullivan.

Library of Congress Cataloging in Publication Data

Sullivan, George, date
   Better cross-country running for boys and girls.

   Summary: An introduction to cross-country running,
including the history of this "natural sport," equip-
ment, training, strategy, and how to improve one's
performance.
   1. Running for children—Juvenile literature.
[1. Running]   I. Title.
GV1061.18.C45S84   1983   796.4'26   83-7208
ISBN 0-396-08172-X

The author is grateful to the many individuals who helped him in the preparation of this book. Special thanks are offered Jim Scott, track coach, St. Francis Xavier High School, New York City, and these members of the Xavier cross-country team who posed for photographs: Chris Nolan, Bill Kelly, Ed Keenan, Ryan Brackley, George Febles, Jim Chopey, and Dan Scott. Special thanks are also due Mimi Fahnestock, the International Running Center Library; Francesca Kurti, T.L.C. Custom Labs; Herb Field, Herb Field Art Studio; Joe Fox, John Devaney, and Aime LaMontagne.

CONTENTS

Start of high school cross-country race at New York's Van Cortlandt Park.

THE NATURAL SPORT

Late every summer, not long after the school semester begins, tens of thousands of young athletes become occupied with cross-country running, an unusual team sport.

Cross-country is running not on a track and not on engineered roads. It is running everywhere else— over gently rolling hills, across green meadows, through woodland paths. It is running in parks, over golf courses, and through school campuses.

The term "cross-country" comes from England. It is an abbreviated version of "cross-countryside," words that perhaps explain the sport more clearly.

Cross-country running is also unique because just about anyone can participate. Unlike basketball, soccer, and softball—sports in which only a limited number can play—cross-country is open to everyone. Virtually every boy or girl who shows up for practice becomes a member of the team.

The cross-country season is short. In most states, it begins in mid-September, continues through October, and reaches a peak in November, when the championship events are held. It is a season that lasts only about eight weeks.

An enormous amount of fun and excitement can be packed into those eight weeks. You're competing with a team and you gain all the benefits that that implies, the sense of belonging, the friendships. There are the challenges and accomplishments.

There's more. Since it involves running in open spaces, cross-country is often called the natural sport. There is less routine, less pressure, as compared to most other sports. Cross-country can mean running for fun.

In the tomb of an Egyptian child, dating to 5200 B.C., toys were discovered that resembled modern bowling pins. That evidence makes bowling one of the oldest of all sports.

But cross-country running is much older. It may be as old as civilized man. Crude forms of footracing date to earliest times, historians say.

The ancient Greeks were well known for the emphasis they placed on sports and games. Legends

Tiring runners drive for the finish.

of incredible feats over the cruelest of terrain have been passed down to us.

Yet it was not until fairly recent times, during the late 1800s, in fact, that cross-country racing began to take on the form and structure it has today. The sport was derived from England. The first account of a cross-country race is contained in a book titled *Athletes and Football*, published in England in 1887. A section of the book written by Walter Rye tells how, at the end of 1867, a few members of the Thames Rowing Club at Putney, of which Rye was a member, decided upon "holding some cross-country steeplechases during the winter season, with the idea of keeping themselves in condition until rowing began again."

Public schools in England are said to have been competing in cross-country at an earlier period, perhaps even before 1837. The sport was also adopted in France, Belgium, and Finland during the nineteenth century.

The earliest date given for organized cross-country competition in the United States is 1890, when the Amateur Athletic Union conducted championship events. The Prospect Harriers of Brooklyn captured the team title that year.

The term "harrier," incidentally, means cross-country runner. It is also a breed of dog, a hound of medium size. Since harriers are used in packs in hunting, it's not hard to understand how the term came to be applied to groups of runners who race in bunches over hill and dale.

The first international cross-country championships were held in England in 1903. Cross-country was an Olympic event in 1912, 1920, and 1924.

The 1912 race, conducted at 8,000 meters (4.9 miles), was won by Hannes Kolehmainen of Finland. His countryman, Paavo Nurmi, won the Olympics cross-country in 1920. The race had been lengthened to 10,000 meters (6.2 miles) that year. Nurmi, called "the Flying Finn" and judged one of the greatest runners of the twentieth century, won the event again in 1924. Cross-country has not been a part of the Olympic program since that date.

Today, competition in high school cross-country is offered in all fifty states. Most school programs offer a series of dual meets in which one team competes against another. Triangular meets, with three teams competing, are also popular.

Teams also take part in invitational runs with competition involving dozens of schools and hundreds of runners. Toward the end of the season, there are likely to be district, sectional, and regional meets. The state finals are scheduled at the very end of the season. In total, a runner might compete in ten or twelve races during a season.

High school teams usually run distances of between two and three miles, although there are some exceptions. Some schools prefer metric measure-

Terrain like this is a feature of most cross-country courses.

Runners tune up for a cross-country race.

ments. In Connecticut and Idaho, for instance, state championships are held over a 5,000-meter course (3.1 miles).

Girls' races are usually shorter than boys' races. In Montana, for example, boys' championships are held at three miles, the girls' at two miles. In Minnesota's state final, the boys run 5,000 meters (3.1 miles), the girls 3,200 meters (2.98 miles).

College men compete at distances of five or six miles, or their approximate metric equivalents, 8,000 or 10,000 meters. College women compete at two miles, three miles, or 5,000 meters (3.1 miles).

Time is relatively unimportant in rating one's performance in a cross-country event. What is important is place, where you finish.

In scoring a cross-country race, you add the places of the first five runners for each team to cross the finish line. The team with the lowest score wins, the team with the second lowest score is second, and so on.

Suppose the first five runners on your team finish 4th, 8th, 31st, 58th, and 102nd. Adding those finishes together, you get a score of 203. If 203 is the lowest score of all, your team is the winner.

Success can thus take many forms in cross-country. You may be able to celebrate your team's victory, or perhaps you'll be good enough to win the race yourself or finish among the leaders.

Your time is relatively unimportant in cross-country. Where you finish is what counts.

Merely placing among the first five runners on your team is reason for applause. Or perhaps you manage to run your personal best time for the course. You can also derive a sense of accomplishment from a spirited kick at the finish that sweeps you past a hard-driving opponent.

Competition in cross-country for high school boys and girls is conducted under rules and regulations set down by the National Federation of State High School Associations (11724 Plaza Circle, Kansas City, MO 64195). Most high schools in the United States are members of the organization.

According to records compiled by the National Federation, the winningest boys' cross-country team in recent years has represented Little Rock Central High School in Little Rock, Arkansas. The Little Rock team captured eighteen state titles in a 24-year period beginning in 1956.

Among girls' high school cross-country teams, the Glasgow Scotties of Glasgow High School in Glasgow, Montana, are among the most successful. The team recently won its seventh state title, most ever for a girls' cross-country team.

Alfred Shrubb was one of the greatest cross-country runners of all time. Almost a century ago, he set cross-country records that lasted for decades.

In a book he wrote about cross-country running, Shrubb spoke of the sport's glories. "There can be nothing superior to cross-country running for either

"There is nothing monotonous in an open country run."

pleasure or health," Shrubb said. "The sport itself is ideal, whether a race be contested in fine or muddy weather. Track or road running are apt to grow monotonous, however exciting they may be; but there is nothing monotonous in an open country run. Even the training itself is almost as enjoyable as the race."

These sentiments are as true today as they were in the 1800s.

14

SHOES AND OTHER EQUIPMENT

The right shoes will not only protect your feet and prevent injury, they can even help to make you a better runner. Inspect all the running shoes you can. Try them on. Run in them if you can.

For cross-country competition, you need *running* shoes. Sneakers, tennis shoes, or basketball shoes won't give your feet the support and protection you need.

Experienced runners distinguish between training flats and racing flats. Most running shoes fit into one or the other of these classifications.

Training flats are basic running flats; they cushion the foot, they cup the heel. They support and stabilize the foot. Racing flats do the same except that they are designed for speed and are lighter in weight. They cost from $10 to $20 more a pair than training flats.

Many runners wear training flats during practice sessions, then switch to racing flats when they compete. Says one runner: "It's the same as with a hitter who swings a weighted baseball bat before he goes up to the plate. When he then swings a bat of standard weight, he can swing it much faster.

"When you wear racing flats in a race after a week of wearing training flats in practice, your feet feel as if they've got wings on them."

These are some of the points you should consider when buying shoes for cross-country:

Fit—Take plenty of time to get the right fit. Don't choose shoes on the basis of color, style, design, or the side-striping they feature. If your shoes don't fit you, you've wasted your money.

Wear your running socks when trying on shoes. If you plan to wear two pairs of socks when you run, as many runners do, be sure to wear them both when trying on shoes.

Once you've donned a pair of shoes and have laced them up, check the toe area carefully. When you run, your foot slides forward in the shoe. Allow about a thumb's width in between the end of your toes and the front of your shoes.

Be certain the shoes are wide enough, too. You should have room to spread out your toes a little. Shoes that are too snug can cause blisters.

Walk around the store in the shoes. Run in place. You want to be sure they're comfortable. Overall, they should feel snug but not tight.

Cushioning—When you run, each foot strikes the ground with about three times the force you use when you're walking. And usually the ground is very hard. Your shoes must act to cushion your foot from this pounding.

Check the sole first. It must not only be thick enough to provide protection and cushioning, it must also be flexible. Most manufacturers accomplish these twin goals by providing soles of two or three layers of rubberized material.

The sole must bend easily when you run. Other-

15

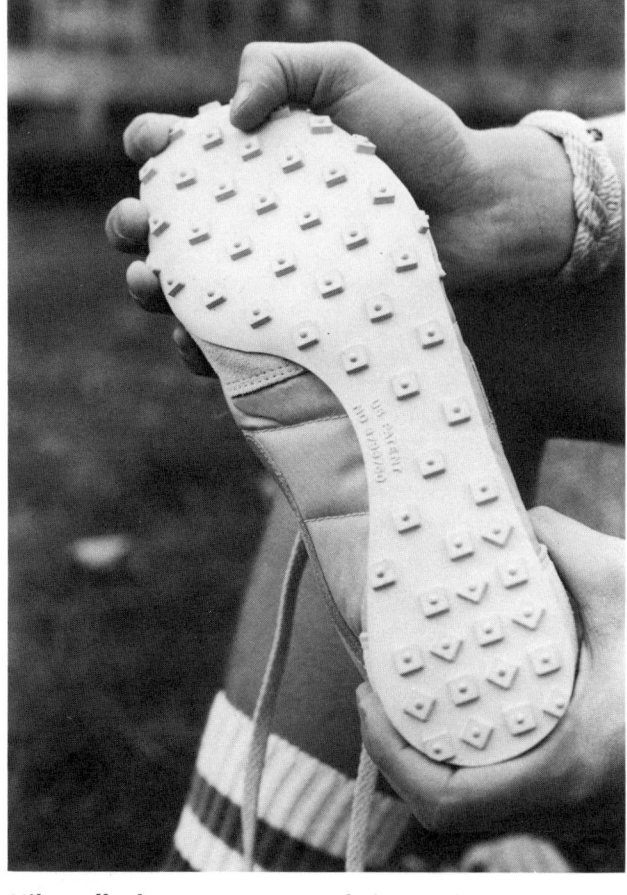

Nike calls these grippers "spikeless spikes."

Also check the heel for cushioning. It has to be extremely resilient to absorb the shock.

TREADS—Shoe treads are especially important in cross-country. They must be able to grip the various types of terrain you're going to encounter—the up-hills and downhills, the grassy fields and forest paths. The treads should also help to cushion your foot on hard surfaces.

Many coaches recommend shoes with studded treads or gridiron patterns. These feature a series of raised grippers designed to provide good traction. The grippers can be round, square, star-shaped, or of almost any other shape. All together, the grippers form a gridiron—or waffle—pattern.

Some cross-country runners prefer to wear spikes. It depends on the terrain. Spikes can be helpful when the footing is bad, but they increase the impact of each step and can give your feet and legs quite a jarring. Be sure to consult your coach before wearing spikes.

During the early 1980s, Nike, Inc. introduced the Waffle Racer for cross-country racing, a shoe the company described as the "spikeless spike." It features square-based grippers that have the ability to cushion the feet on hard surfaces and provide traction on soft surfaces. It has a snug fit and is extremely light in weight.

THE HEEL—Sturdy construction in the rear-foot area of the shoes is also very important. Otherwise, the shoes won't give your feet the stability they require.

wise your feet will suffer. Before you try on the shoes, try bending the front part of the sole back and forth to be sure it's flexible.

16

Plenty of rear-foot stability and sturdy heel counter make these running shoes (called Phaetons) excellent for cross-country.

Check the shoes to determine that the top of the heel hits the back of your foot at a comfortable level. If it hits too high, you're sure to develop blisters. If it strikes too low, it can mean you're not getting enough support.

Also examine the heel counter, the section at the back of the heel that protects the Achilles tendon, the tendon that joins the calf muscles to the heel bone. The counter should be firm yet comfortable.

THE UPPERS—The upper is the part of the shoe above the sole. It should give good support and be long lasting. The manufacturer's distinctive markings appear on each side of the upper.

In good running shoes, the uppers are nylon or leather or a combination of the two. Many runners prefer nylon uppers because they are light in weight, water resistant, and permit air circulation.

Whichever material you decide upon, choose

Lacing system of this shoe (the Arizona) gives added stability to rear-foot area.

uppers that are soft inside and firm enough to give your foot stability. Avoid uppers with heavy seams that can cause chafing.

How long should a pair of running shoes last? It depends on many factors—the quality of the shoes, the surface on which you usually run, your body weight, and your running style. But, in general, figure a pair of running shoes should last for about 500 miles.

CLOTHING FOR CROSS-COUNTRY—Once you've selected your running shoes, the rest is easy. Indeed, if you become a member of your school team, your running outfit is likely to be furnished by the school.

You'll be provided with "sweats," an outfit consisting of cotton sweat pants and a pullover cotton sweat shirt. Sweats prevent you from getting a chill.

It's never wise to wear a running suit of rubberized, plastic, or other nonporous material. Running on a warm day in such an outfit can cause your body heat to build to a dangerous level, leading to muscle cramps, dehydration, and even heat exhaustion.

Give some thought about what to wear when the weather turns very hot or very cold.

On extremely hot days, wear as little as possible. Nylon or cotton running shorts are recommended, with nylon the more comfortable of the two. Since cotton absorbs more perspiration, and because the seams are likely to be bulkier and heavier, it can cause chafing.

But cotton is the best material for the upper body. It feels cool because it absorbs perspiration, which evaporates as you run.

A white shirt reflects the heat much better than a dark-colored one. Wear a wide-brimmed hat or baseball cap to keep the sun off your head.

In cold weather, the best policy is to wear clothes in layers. The air gets trapped in between each layer and acts as additional insulation.

Don a cotton undershirt and long johns first, then a light wool sweater and shorts. If it's exceptionally cold, you can add another layer consisting of a heavier sweater or Windbreaker plus sweat pants.

Be careful not to overdress, however. Wear just enough to keep yourself warm.

Be sure to protect your head, wrists, and hands on very cold days. As much as 40 percent of the body's heat escapes through your head. Cover up with a wool knit hat or hooded sweat shirt.

Mittens, not gloves, give your hands the best protection.

On cold days, be aware of the direction in which the wind is blowing. Start your run by heading into the wind; you'll warm up by running. On your return, you'll have the wind at your back to push you along.

WARMING UP

Always warm up. Before every training session and race, take the time to stretch your muscles and get your heart and lungs pumping. Some experts say that as many as half of the strains, sprains, and other injuries related to running could have been avoided if the victim had taken the time to warm up properly.

Spend 10 to 15 minutes warming up. However, exactly how much stretching and loosening up you do depends to a great extent on your own physical characteristics. Some runners require more stretching than others. Says one coach: "Let your body tell you how long to warm up, how much to stretch." This means you should be alert to signs of fatigue that indicate you're overstretching. Too much stretching can be as bad as too little.

Some runners use a medicated lotion or ointment, such as Ben-Gay, to help them warm up, applying it to the leg muscles. Such medications are also used to help avoid muscle tightness, especially on cold days. But many coaches feel that these preparations aren't necessary if you spend sufficient time and effort stretching.

The exercises pictured and described in this section are among those that coaches recommend for distance runners.

LEG STRETCH—This is a simple exercise, the aim of which is to stretch the muscles of the ankle, calf,

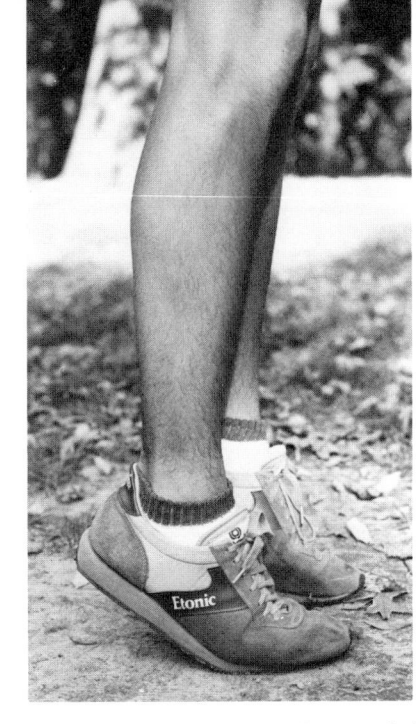

Rise up on your toes, then rock back on your heels. This exercise stretches the muscles of the ankles, calves, and thighs.

and thigh. Use it to begin your warm-up session.

Stand erect, your hands at your thighs, your feet about 12 inches apart.

Rise up on your toes, hold the pose briefly, and return to the starting position.

Then rock back on your heels, hold it, then return to the starting position again. Repeat the exercise several times.

The "step-in-place" exercise is also good for loosening up the leg muscles.

STEP IN PLACE—This is another exercise with which to begin your warm-up drill. It's good for the muscles at the front and back of the leg and the Achilles tendon, the tendon at the back of the heel.

Stand erect, your hands at your sides, and place your right foot in front of your left. There should be about 12 inches separating the back of the right heel and the toe of your left shoe.

Keeping your left foot flat to the ground and left leg straight, bend your right knee. You'll feel the muscle tension at the back of the left leg and foot. Hold the position briefly, then return to the start.

Repeat the exercise with the left foot forward and the right foot back.

TORSO STRETCH—You flex the muscles of your upper body, particularly the back, shoulder, and neck muscles, with this simple drill.

Stand erect, your feet about 12 inches apart, and your arms extended out to your sides.

Keeping the arms extended, turn the upper body as far to the left as you can without causing any undue strain, hold it, and then turn your upper body to the right. Repeat the drill several times.

HAMSTRING STRETCH—The hamstrings are the tendons at the back or hollow, of the knee. The term also refers to the muscle at the back of the thigh and knee. You'll feel the hamstrings flex when you do this exercise.

Stand erect and cross one foot in front of the other. Keeping your legs straight, bend forward

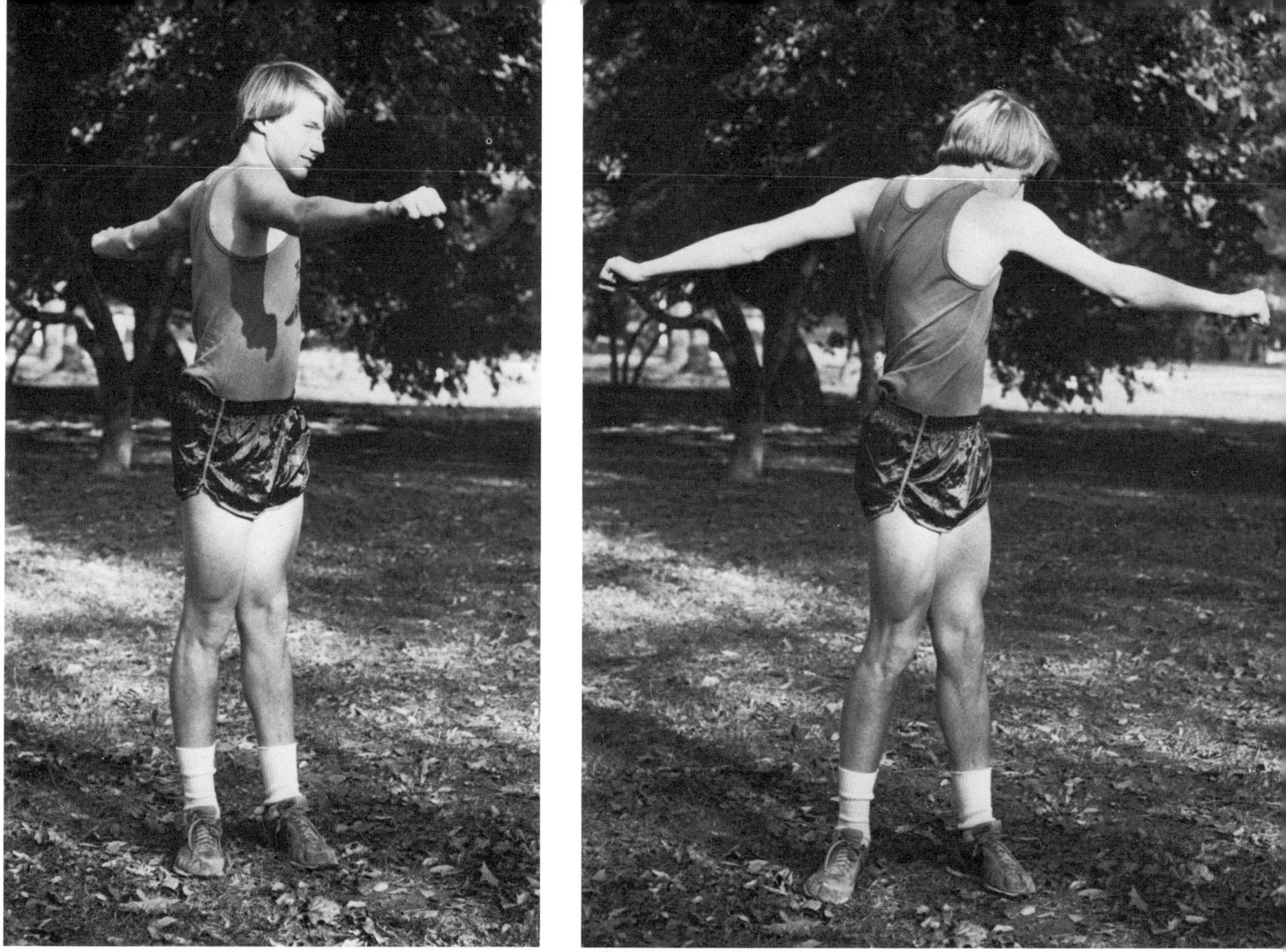

Twisting the upper body in one direction and then the other is simple
but effective in stretching the muscles of the neck, back, and shoulder.

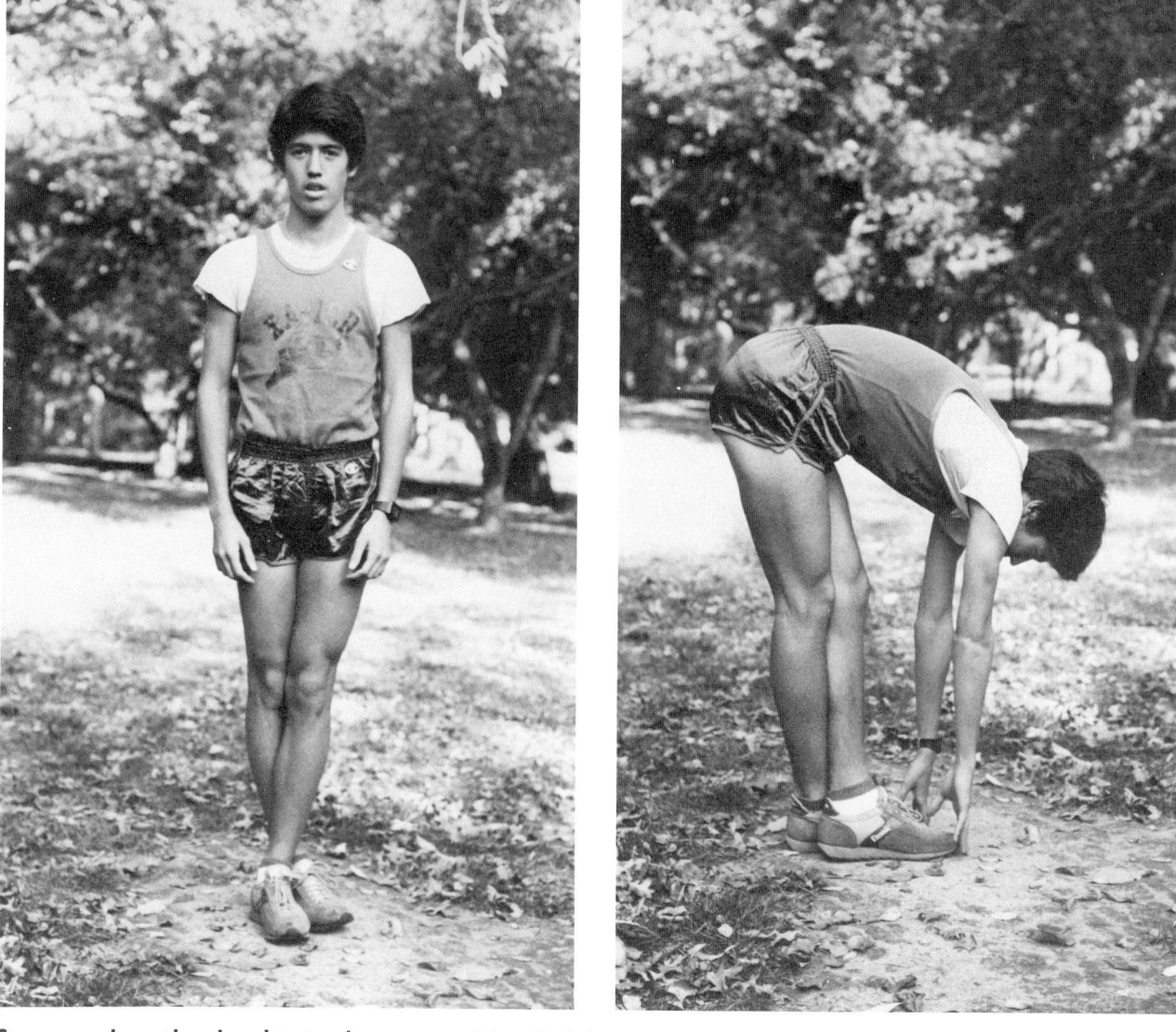

Cross your legs, then bend to touch your toes. It's called the hamstring stretch.

This is also good for stretching the leg muscles, but you need a park bench.

Virtually all distance runners, not just cross-country enthusiasts, perform the push-away.

slowly from the waist and touch your toes. Hold the position for a few seconds, then reverse the position of your feet, and repeat the drill.

LEG STRETCH—You need a park bench or other similar object to perform this exercise. Face the bench and raise your right leg to the back of the bench (or to the seat, if that level feels more convenient).

Then reach forward slowly with both hands toward the toes of the elevated leg. When you have reached as far as you can without straining, hold the position for a few seconds. Then reverse legs and repeat the drill.

PUSH-AWAY—This is an exercise almost everyone performs before a race. Begin by facing a wall, tree, or some other stationary object. Your feet should be flat to the ground, your toes pointing toward the tree.

This isn't easy to do but it's very efficient in stretching the muscles of the lower back. Notice that as the feet go back, the hands go back, too.

Keeping your heels to the ground and your body straight, lean toward the tree and press your palms upon it. Bend your elbows and press hard. You should feel muscle pressure at the front of your thighs and the back of your legs. If you don't feel pressure, you are probably too close to the tree; move back a few inches and try again.

Hold the position for two or three seconds. Repeat the drill several times.

BACK STRETCH—Lie on your back and raise your

feet over your head while keeping your legs straight. Your hands go back, too. Repeat the exercise several times.

HURDLER'S STRETCH—This is another exercise you'll see at every meet. Your body position resembles that of an athlete leaping over a hurdle.

Sit on the ground with your right leg extended. Fold the left leg back, tucking the foot beside the buttocks. Your hands are at your sides.

Reach forward and touch your right foot, bending forward at the waist to do so. Repeat the exercise several times. Then do the drill with the left leg extended and the right leg folded back.

You flex the muscles of the back, thigh, lower leg, and belly when you perform the hurdler's stretch.

You should also spend some time cooling down after you run. A few minutes of light calisthenic exercises, such as those described here, and some light jogging will help your body return to its normal physical state.

Thus, every cross-country experience should be a three-part cycle, involving warming up, the run itself, and cooling down. It's the healthful way to enjoy the sport.

Hurdler's stretch is another runners' favorite.

YOUR RUNNING FORM

Everyone knows how to run. Everyone can run pretty fast and pretty far.

But when you have to run two miles or more, as you do in a cross-country race, it's different. You're putting your feet and legs through a tough test. If you fail to stride correctly, you can't expect to do well. Problems can result and you can even injure yourself. Good running form is very important.

This doesn't mean you should study the photographs in this section and try to copy them exactly. Everyone has his or her own running style. Some kids are tall and slim and run with ease and grace. Others are short and stocky, yet they're able to run fast and cover long distances.

The heel of your foot should come down first, landing softly. Roll your foot forward and push off from the toes. Pump your arms easily.

You must develop your own running style. It should be a style that enables you to be relaxed when you run and move efficiently.

The guidelines set down on the pages that follow will help you to become a relaxed and efficient runner. Follow them in developing your own running style.

FOOTPLANT—Distance running is much the same as walking. On each step, the heel of your foot should touch the ground first, landing softly. Then roll forward on the foot and push off from the toes.

Don't run the way sprinters run. Sprinters land on their toes or on the balls of their feet. Sprinters' heels almost never touch the track during a race. But to run on one's toes for a long distance would cause severe muscle cramps.

Some runners land flat-footed. Their feet "slap" the ground as they stride. It's difficult to run very fast or far for an extended period using this style.

It's also wrong to land too far back on the heel, hitting the ground with the foot rigid instead of relaxed.

Your foot should always come down lightly and silently, the heel touching first. Gently roll forward onto the ball of your foot, and then push off from the toes.

THE STRIDE—The length of your stride is directly related to your build. The taller you are, the longer your stride. Length of stride is also related to pace. The faster the pace, the longer your stride.

You should seek to develop a natural stride that feels comfortable. Keeping your knees slightly bent as you run will help you in attaining a natural stride.

Beware of overstriding. Don't thrust your knees forward and kick back with your feet as you run. In other words, don't bounce along.

You can get some idea of the character of your stride by examining the soles of a pair of well-worn running shoes. If, for example, the forward part of each shoe shows a considerable amount of wear, it is likely to be a sign that you're landing more toward the ball of your foot.

The sole of each of your running shoes should display even wear over the entire surface. That's one sign that your stride is a good one.

YOUR POSTURE—"Run tall"—that's what coaches often tell their runners.

Running tall means to run upright. It means to run with your upper body erect.

Running tall, however, doesn't mean that your body position should be the same as a soldier on parade. Although your back should be straight and your chin up, you shouldn't lock your back and chin into these positions. Your body should never be rigid.

YOUR ARMS AND HANDS—Pump your arms easily as you run, keeping your hands close to your body. Your elbows should be flexed at about a 90-degree angle, but don't make your arm position rigid. Keep your arms relaxed.

Your hands should be lightly closed, the fingers just touching the palms. Never make a tight fist.

YOUR SHOULDERS—Try to keep your shoulders level.

BREATHING—There is a theory that states that a runner should breathe in through the nose and breathe out through the mouth. Forget it. If you try this method of breathing, you'll severely limit your intake of air and won't remain among the leaders for very long. Open up your mouth and devour all the air you can get.

This is a proper way to breathe, and it is as important to distance running as the right posture and keeping relaxed. It's called belly breathing.

Most people breathe from the chest. They suck

their bellies in when they inhale. But this is not an efficient way to breathe.

When you breathe correctly, your belly expands as you breathe in and flattens when you breathe out. This indicates that you're inflating your lungs to their utmost, that you're breathing efficiently.

Try belly breathing—expanding your belly on every inhale and flattening it when you exhale. It's

Breathe through your mouth as well as your nose.

No two people have exactly the same running style. You have to develop your own.

a good way to breathe all the time, not merely when you're running.

To determine whether you've mastered the art, try this test: lie on your back and place a book (one that's about twice as heavy as this one) on your belly. Take a deep breath. If you're belly breathing, the book will rise.

You may encounter some runners who time their breathing with their footplants. For example, a runner may inhale every time his or her left foot strikes the ground, and exhale when each right foot goes down.

Should you try this breathing technique? Most coaches say no. You have enough to be concerned about during a race without worrying about timing your breathing. Simply learn to belly breathe, and then inhale and exhale at a rate that is natural for you.

A final word: No one can tell you what your running style should be. You were born with certain characteristics in your manner of walking and running that are never going to change very much.

You can overcome certain bad habits you may have developed. You can learn to stop running on your toes. You can overcome a tendency to over-stride. You can learn to "run tall," pumping your arms easily.

But aside from these simple mechanics, running should be natural. Simply be yourself when you run.

SURVEYING THE COURSE

Your strategy for a race depends to some extent on the type of course you're going to be running. That means you should inspect the course carefully before the race.

Don't depend on someone else to tell you about the course. That's like having someone describe a television program they have seen. To get to know what it's really like—all the details—you have to see the program yourself.

Your coach is likely to provide you and your teammates with sufficient time to jog over the course, perhaps as a tune-up the day before the race. Be a careful observer during this run. Here are some of the questions you should seek to answer:

- How long are the opening and closing sections?
- How is the footing?
- Are there sharp turns?
- Are there narrow pathways?
- Are there hills? How long are they? How steep?
- Is the route clearly marked?

If any part of the course seems particularly troublesome, go back and study it again.

When you travel to a distant town for competition, arriving only an hour or two before the race, there may not be any opportunity to survey the entire course. But inspect as much of it as you can.

You've heard of home-court advantage in basket-

Be sure to survey the hills—where they're to be found and their steepness.

31

ball. Well, in cross-country running, there's a home-*course* advantage. Unless you and your teammates become familiar with the terrain you're going to be covering, you can easily fall victim to it.

Some cross-country courses and races have become nationally famous. There's the Mount San Antonio College Cross-Country Meet in California, offering races for colleges, junior colleges, high schools, junior high schools, grade schools, and "open" contestants, that is, individuals who do not belong to any special class of competitors. It's a three-day event with much of the same hoopla as a Mardi Gras. More than 6,000 runners take part in the festivities.

Almost as big is the annual cross-country meet sponsored by Manhattan College and contested over

New York's Van Cortlandt Park attracts thousands of runners every week of the cross-country season.

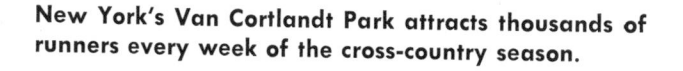

Does the course contain a paved stretch? Make note of its location and length.

the hills, wooded pathways, and open fields of New York City's Van Cortlandt Park. In one recent year, the event attracted 5,900 runners from 241 schools in eight states.

Van Cortlandt Park, incidentally, at the northern edge of New York's borough of the Bronx, has a rich history as a mecca for cross-country runners of the Northeast. It is convenient to several highways and turnpikes. Bus and subway transportation lead to the park. Van Cortlandt plays host to more than a hundred dual meets a year and scores of invitational and championship meets as well.

The many thousands of runners who compete there try to break the 13:00 mark for the 2.5-mile high school course, and 25:00 for the five-mile college course. The high school record is 12:16.4, set in 1975 by Luis Ostolozaga, who represented Bishop Loughlin High School in Brooklyn.

Although located in New York City, Van Cortlandt Park has its woodsy stretches.

Runners get off to a good start in an important sectional race.

THE START

Because most cross-country races are run at distances of two miles and more, the start is not as critical as in a sprint. Nevertheless, it is important to get away fast, to be among the leaders from the instant the gun sounds.

This is especially true if you happen to be one of the better runners in a race. You want to be able to run at your own pace. By exploding away at the start, you avoid getting snarled in heavy traffic.

Keep relaxed in the moments before the start. If you begin to feel tense, run in place or do some light jogging, covering thirty or forty yards.

In the minutes before the start, runners get instructions from the starter.

In the standing start, place one foot just in back of the starting line, the other foot to the rear. When the gun goes off, explode away.

Cross-country runners use a standing start. Not only does the standing start serve to get you away fast, but it also provides you with the stability needed in a race with scores of competitors where you can easily get bumped at the start.

Two signals are usually used in starting a cross-country race—a whistle and a gun.

The whistle is a signal to get set. When the whistle sounds, get in position behind the starting line. Place one foot just in back of the line, the other foot to the rear. Bend your knees slightly and bend from the waist, eyeing the horizon. Let your hands hang loosely at your sides. Your weight should be concentrated on your front foot.

When the gun goes off, drive off your rear foot. Get your arms pumping. Keep driving hard. Once you're free of the pack, settle into your normal pace.

Many cross-country races are laid out in such a way that the trails and hilly portions are sandwiched between opening and closing stretches of flat terrain. Getting out in front fast is vital when competing on such a course. If you should fall behind in the early stages, you put yourself at a disadvantage. You're not likely to be able to pass the slower runners and catch the leaders along the crowded pathways that wind through the hills.

In important regional or sectional races, the starting line may be swarming with runners. Because of the crowding, you may catch an elbow in the ribs

You should strive to be among the leaders by the time you reach the course's narrow pathways and hills.

or get shouldered to one side at the start. Be prepared for such jolts and don't let them upset you. Keep your mind on getting to the front.

Coach and runners map strategy before a cross-country race.

RACE STRATEGY AND TACTICS

Every time you enter a cross-country race, you should establish an objective for yourself. It can be a higher place finish or a faster time for the course. Or you can make defeating a certain opponent your goal.

But don't set a goal that's unrealistic. You'll only end up discouraging yourself.

One of your goals might be to run five seconds faster on your home course than you've ever run

before. Allow yourself two or three meets to reach this goal. If you don't achieve it in those two or three meets, keep trying.

Always remember that you're going to experience highs and lows as a runner. There will be days when you feel absolutely unbeatable. There will be other days when you feel like you're carrying a small child on your back. You must learn to accept poor performances once in a while. They happen to the best of runners.

Track coaches throughout the country realize that cross-country competition is an excellent conditioner for their middle-distance and distance runners and even for sprinters. Thus, many runners who take part in cross-country are primarily athletes in training for other events.

If you are in this category, always be sure to concentrate on doing your best. Don't dismiss a poor performance by saying, "I'm only out to get in shape for track." Such lack of motivation could easily carry over to your track program. Approach each cross-country race with the same competitive instincts you bring to sprinting or distance running.

PRERACE MEAL—If you talk to twelve different runners, you'll get a dozen different theories about what to eat before a race and when to eat it. Some encourage strict fasting. Others promote "carbohydrate loading," that is, eating large amounts of carbohydrate-rich foods—spaghetti, pizza, pancakes, bread, potatoes, cake, and ice cream—in the days before a race. Carbohydrates are believed to build up energy reserves.

Much of what is said and written about runners' diets is controversial. But coaches, trainers, and diet experts agree it's always best to run on an empty stomach.

Most young runners can't imagine going without breakfast the morning of a race. There's nothing wrong with breakfast. Just be sure that any prerace meal is light. As one nutritionist has put it, "No one has ever gotten fast by eating." Don't eat anything at all for two or three hours before the race.

It's not just that running on a full stomach is unpleasant, it can also slow you down. After you eat, the body sends extra blood to the stomach to aid the digestive process. The blood that is working on digestion is unavailable to carry oxygen to the muscles, which are demanding an increased amount of it. The result is that you tire more easily than you would if you hadn't eaten.

Also be careful about the kinds of foods you eat in any prerace meal. Certain foods and beverages can upset your stomach once you start running, fruit, milk, and coffee among them.

Carbohydrate loading is a subject that's frequently discussed nowadays. Many long-distance runners swear by this eating method.

The theory is that by stuffing yourself with carbohydrate-rich foods for two or three days before a race, you build the amount of glycogen stored in the muscles to an above average level. Glycogen is a major source of energy anytime the body puts forth an intense effort. When the glycogen reserves run out, fatigue sets in.

Carbohydrate loading doesn't work for every runner. And it has no benefit unless the physical effort is actually going to use up your supply of glycogen, which requires running two hours or so. Loading up for a cross-country race which lasts only about fifteen minutes isn't going to help you.

There are no magic diets or miracle foods that are going to help you become a cross-country champion. The "secret" to improving is to eat a well-balanced diet. That means three meals a day that provide sufficient proteins, carbohydrates, fats, vitamins, minerals, and water. It's as simple as that.

PACE—You won't be involved in running for very long before you develop a sense of pace. That is, you'll learn to run certain distances at measured speeds. For example, your coach, once he or she has come to know you as a runner, may recommend that you run a 5:30 mile once during each practice session. Or your coach may recommend that you run two miles in 12:00.

During a race, time in itself is not a valid criterion. Your time for a mile may be the fastest of your life, but if you happened to have run it over mostly downhill terrain, your record doesn't mean very much.

Time in a cross-country can only be taken as a performance gauge when it is related to a fixed loca-

When you move to pass an opponent, go all out. Try to leave him far behind.

tion. For instance, on your home course, it may be a well-known fact that you and your teammates should always try to arrive at a certain bridge at 4:40. Your coach is likely to have an assistant posted on the bridge with a timer who announces your time as you flit by. You then know whether you're maintaining your pace, whether you should slow down or speed up. There may be two or three such checkpoints during a race.

You should always pace yourself during a race.

It doesn't make any sense to run the first part of a race with the leaders but end finishing with the tail-enders. Nor does it do any good to get involved in a personal duel with rival runners early in the race if you become so fatigued that you can't launch a strong finish. By pacing yourself, you can avoid such lapses.

PASSING OPPONENTS—Your goal should be to pass each rival in turn. Don't try to do too much at any one time. If you're in eighth position in a race, your task should be to move up to seventh, then sixth, and so on. If you're in seventy-eighth position, your aim should be to take over seventy-seventh position, then seventy-sixth, then seventy-fifth.

When you do pass, turn on the speed. Move out. Leave your rival in the dust. You don't want your opponent to get the idea that he or she can recover, turn on some speed, and pass *you*. You want your opponent to feel defeated, even discouraged.

Pulling away after you've passed an opponent can also boost your confidence. You'll feel more encouraged to roll along and pass the next runner.

COPING WITH THE WIND—Head winds and tail winds can be a big factor in a race. Strong head winds are tough. A head wind of 10 miles an hour can cut your speed as much as 5 percent.

When you encounter a stiff head wind and it appears you will be running into it for an extended time, lean into it, bending from the hips. It may also help if you shorten your strides a bit. Or try ducking in behind another runner or group of runners. Let them break the wind for you.

A tail wind is a blessing. A tail wind of 10 miles an hour will boost your speed by about 3 percent. You just have to have the stamina to handle the faster pace at which your legs will be moving.

CORNERING—Taking corners is something few runners give much thought to, but if you're skilled in the art you can gain as much as half a stride on an opponent. This can be a critical advantage in a close race.

Prepare for the turn several strides before you reach it. Move your outside shoulder forward; your inside shoulder goes back.

As you reach the turn, lean into it and bring your legs into alignment with your shoulders. Keep your feet moving. You'll zip around the corner like a kid on a bicycle.

RUNNING IN A PACK—Some coaches instruct their runners to run in groups, in packs, for at least part of the race. This strategy can give a team a psychological advantage. For one thing, the runners can offer words of encouragement to one another. Bunching, as it is also called, can be a big help to the weaker runners.

Racing in a pack can cause problems for the opposition. When a runner gets passed by four or five opponents all at once, it can be very discouraging.

If your team is facing a particularly strong opponent, or if the outcome of the race seems as if it is going to be determined by the final finishing places, you and your teammates may be called upon to box in a runner. In so doing, you hem in, block, or surround the opponent, so that he or she must slow down or go wide to pass. An outstanding runner is likely to outrun or outfight the box, of course, but the strategy serves to delay or tire the victim.

Two, three, or four runners can be used in constructing a box. When two runners are used, they run side by side and just in front of the opponent.

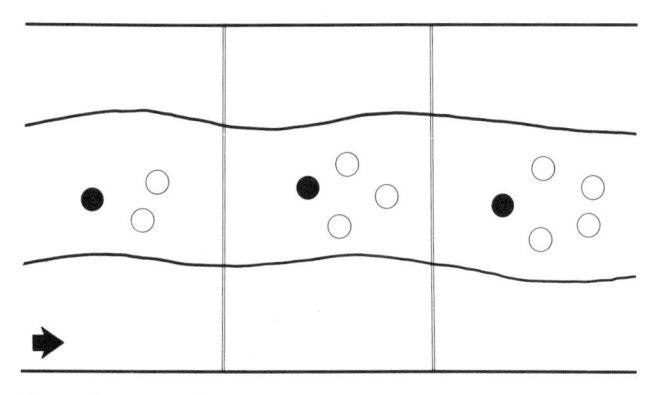

Two, three, or four runners can team up to box in a rival.

In the case of a three-runner box, the formation is the same with the addition of a lead runner.

The four-runner box is sometimes called a group box. There are two runners at each elbow of the opponent and two in front.

The runners' positions in the box may change as the terrain changes. Then, as the race enters its final stages, it's up to the box runners to decide when to forsake the box and make an all-out sprint for the tape.

Matching up is another race tactic your team may use. Matching up is common to dual meets. Your coach will assign you and each of your teammates an opposing runner to run against. Your task is not to allow that runner to pass you.

As these paragraphs suggest, there can be body contact in cross-country, especially in large fields when runners get crowded together. Be prepared for some give and take. Someone may jar you with

Crowded starts provide opportunity for jostling.

Runners drive for good finishing positions in race's final stages.

a shoulder. You may catch an elbow in the ribs. An opponent may step on your heel.

Usually such contact is accidental. But sometimes it's not; it results from being aggressive.

Suppose you're in the final straightaway leading to the finish line and the chute, where the order of finish is recorded. You're going strong, passing one tired runner after another.

But as you approach the chute, a cluster of runners is blocking your path. Should you slow down and trail them to the finish? Not at all. Plow right through them. There may be several points for your team involved.

You may bruise a few people and tempers may flare, but there are times in cross-country when you must go on the attack, be aggressive, and this is one of them.

THE FINISH—As you reach the final stages of the race, turn on your remaining speed and zip across the finish line. Never slow down as you approach or cross the line. In virtually every cross-country race, there are instances of runners being nipped at the finish line because they faltered. Always think in terms of finishing the race two or three yards beyond the line.

You should be at the peak of exhaustion as you cross the line, without an ounce of energy left. If you're not completely exhausted, you haven't run to your full potential.

UPHILL AND DOWNHILL

Slopes, grades, and outright hills are a feature of every cross-country course. You have to be able to approach each with confidence, and ascend and descend them with efficiency and speed. Cross-country races are often decided on the hills.

You have to modify your running stride a bit when going uphill and downhill, particularly uphill. As you approach the hill, maintain your pace and lean into the hill.

For a short, steep hill, shorten your stride and raise your knees higher. Get up on your toes more, springing forward. Pump your arms in exaggerated fashion.

Maintain your upright posture. Don't hunch over or bend at the waist. Keep your chin up. Look seven or eight feet ahead.

Run smoothly. Run relaxed. Don't clench your hands into fists. Don't tighten your shoulders or jaw. Doing so will wreck your speed.

While it's important to attack the hill when you ascend, you don't want to attack it with such fury that you arrive at the top exhausted. You want to have enough energy remaining to be able to take off on the downhill side. That's when you can really fly.

"Some runners die on the uphills," says one coach. "Then when they get to the top and start down, they don't have anything left. They're not

In attacking a hill, get up on your toes more. Pump . . .

46

. . . your arms vigorously. Be sure to keep your upright posture.

On downhills, open up. Keep in control . . .

able to use the momentum generated by the down-hill slope to their advantage. The uphill actually destroys them twice."

Once you do start downhill, don't lean back. The key is to keep your hips positioned over your feet at all times.

48

. . . but lengthen your stride to take advantage of the momentum the slope provides.

Your leg action will be faster than normal. Your strides will be longer. Be sure to lift your knees. Otherwise, a foot may brush the surface of the hill and cause you to fall. Your arms will pump faster to keep in rhythm with your legs.

If the hill is particularly steep, hit down a little

49

harder on your heels. This will brake your forward motion.

The key to successful downhill running is control. If you go too fast, you will use up too much energy. You also will run the risk of straining a muscle or falling.

Going too slowly can also be hazardous. When you lean forward and seek to brake your forward speed, as many beginners do, you put a severe strain on your thigh muscles. You also lose time.

For each hill, you have to find a happy medium. You want to stay in control, keep relaxed, yet move at the greatest possible speed.

Much of your cross-country training will involve hill running. You are sure to find this very demanding, for it requires muscles that you don't use to a great extent when running on flat terrain.

But uphill and downhill running provide special benefits. When you run uphill, you stimulate your cardiovascular system, that is, your heart and lungs. Constant stimulation of the cardiovascular system strengthens your heart and it becomes a more efficient pump. Stronger lungs mean that you can take in a greater amount of air with each breath. Your body also becomes better able to distribute oxygen through the lungs into the bloodstream. All of this means that you have greater stamina. You can run faster and farther without tiring.

Running uphill also helps you to strengthen the quadriceps, the large muscles at the front of the thighs. The quadriceps are important in developing a powerful stride. Training only on level ground does little toward strengthening the quadriceps.

Running downhill is just as important. It forces you to concentrate on improving your stride. It improves your ability to move your legs fast when you're highly relaxed. Russian track coaches are known to have improved the speed of their sprinters dramatically by having them train on downhill courses.

If you're just beginning hill training, approach it with some caution. Your first workouts should be scheduled on a gentle hill. Run at a rate of speed that is not going to place great stress on your legs.

While you may feel exhilarated after a hill workout and want to do more, be careful. The muscle tightness and soreness that may result can last for several days, forcing you to forego your regular training.

Hill work is perhaps the best training there is for cross-country running. But be sure to approach hills defensively and develop your program gradually.

TRAINING

Dear ———,

I hope you're enjoying your summer vacation. Now that August has arrived, it's time to start thinking of the cross-country season. I'm enclosing a copy of our meet schedule.

I hope you've already begun training. If you have, I'd like you to increase the length of your workouts and add to your weekly mileage. By the end of the month, you should be covering six to eight miles a day five or six times a week. You should also be doing some hill work at least once a week.

If you have any questions about your program, please call me. I'd like to hear what progress you're making.

I hope you're as enthusiastic about the season ahead as I am. I look forward to seeing you in September.

Sincerely,

Robert Tippett
Coach, Cross-Country

If you're a member of a cross-country team, you've probably received a letter something like this one. As the letter suggests, there is no vacation from training during the summer. Cross-country runners work the year-round to keep in condition.

Hill work is included in every training program.

51

Many different types of training methods are used. Fartlek drills are common. "Fartlek" is a Swedish word that means "speed play." When you take part in a fartlek drill you run over different types of terrain at different speeds, from an all-out sprint to a slow jog.

The fartlek work may be programmed for a specific period of time, one hour, say. During that period, you might run four 50-yard sprints, four 440-yard runs, a 50-yard uphill course, and a 50-yard downhill course. You'd jog between each of these runs. The entire workout might cover seven or eight miles.

Pace work is another common training technique for cross-country. When you do pace work, you're expected to run a specific distance, two miles for instance, at a specific speed. Or the coach may suggest you run a total of 40 to 50 miles each week, maintaining a 6:00 or 6:30 pace for each mile.

Another theory of training stresses running long distances at a relatively slow pace. This method is called long slow distance, or LSD, for short. "Train slower, race faster," is the motto of those who support this theory.

While LSD work can be important, it's just as important not to run too many miles. Some coaches say no high school runner should run more than 60 miles a week. Others say the amount should be less, no more than 40 or 50 miles a week. There is a limit to what you can do and it's harmful to go beyond it.

Interval training is conducted on a track. You run . . .

Uphill and downhill running are part of every cross-country training program. However, since hill work is so fatiguing, it is usually scheduled only once or twice a week.

There is also interval training, which is usually conducted on a track. For example, you may be

. . . your fastest over measured sprint distances.

called on to run four timed 440s, or two timed 880s —or do both.

Interval training can take many forms. It depends on the coach's recommendations.

What type of training should you be doing? It's up to you to discuss the subject with your coach and develop a program that suits your experience, talent, and temperament.

Craig Virgin of Lebanon, Illinois, who later lived in Oregon and who won several national cross-country championships, echoed the belief of many coaches when he once said that high school runners

Craig Virgin—"I watched. I listened. I learned."

should develop their own training routines. "When I was in high school, that's what I did," Virgin said. "I watched. I listened. I learned. I adapted what others were doing, experimenting until I found a program that suited my personality and my physical characteristics.

"I ran from 60 to 80 miles a week, blending quality and quantity. Some runners I knew were running more than that, others less. But it didn't matter— that's what worked for me.

"The high school I went to didn't have a track, so I measured one out on the grass and another one on an asphalt road. That's where I did my training. You just have to adapt."

In developing your program, keep in mind that training for cross-country involves three phases: preseason, early season, and sharpening.

Preseason training is summertime training. It's what you do to prepare your body for the more rigorous training and competition. It's foundation work. Preseason training emphasizes distance running at a specific pace, usually on a daily basis.

Early-season training also includes distance work, but at a faster pace. Overall, there's more intensity to the program. You are likely to get involved in hill running, mile runs at a specific speed, or even some speed work.

To sharpen your skills even more, to reach peak condition, your coach is likely to advise you to reduce the number of miles you've been running each week, but to run them at a faster pace. Interval work becomes more important.

In refining your program, you may be aided by

The Harrier (8347 Island Lake Road, Dexter, MI 48130), a newsletter devoted to cross-country which is published ten times a year. *The Harrier* offers training tips and discloses the training programs followed by leading cross-country runners. A one-year subscription costs $10.

Your training program should never become drudgery. Be sure to arrange to take some time off during the year. Some runners take a three- or four-week vacation from running at the end of the season. One coach instructs his runners to skip running for the entire month of July.

What's said in this section applies to girls as well as boys. A case in point is Norway's Grete Waitz, one of the best cross-country runners of all time. Her victory record in international cross-country competition is unsurpassed. She also distinguished herself with frequent victories in the New York Marathon and other celebrated events.

"I remember very well the first time I ran longer than 100 meters [109 yards]," she once recalled. "It was a cross-country race over 400–500 meters [about 440 yards, or one quarter of a mile]. I was 13 years old. I finished first."

After that triumph, Waitz began training four to six times a week. "I never ran longer than 8 to 10 kilometers [10 kilometers is equal to 6.2 miles]," she once told an interviewer. "On the track, I ran intervals of 150 to 400 meters."

Since Waitz also competed in outdoor track, her

Norway's Grete Waitz established new training standards for women.

workouts often stressed speed more than distance. During the winter she trained in the city streets of her native Oslo long before daybreak because the deep snow prevented her from running in the woods. She averaged 120 to 140 kilometers (74.6 to 87 miles) per week.

In the spring, she began running in the woods again. She also did speed training at least four times a week. Summer brought track season and so Grete reduced the number of miles she logged each week but increased the pace of her track workouts.

It was a year-round grind. Patti Catalano, one of the finest American distance runners, once said of Waitz, "She made girls realize that they can't work out like girls. They have to work out like athletes."

Stretching out, increasing the length of your stride, may help you to run faster.

You may be able to improve your speed by making your legs move faster.

HOW TO IMPROVE

Month by month, season by season, you should show steady improvement as a runner. The fact that your body is developing and getting stronger helps to assure this. This section offers advice on how to accelerate that improvement.

Increasing the length of your running stride may help you to become a faster runner. It doesn't have to be a big increase, merely an inch or two. Work on this change during your summertime practice sessions, certainly not during the season.

But you must guard against overstriding. You lose your normal push and drive when you overstride, and your speed is reduced as a result.

Your rate of leg movement is another factor that affects how fast you run. If you can learn to move your legs faster, yet not shorten your stride, you

Good running posture is essential for good speed.

should be able to become a faster runner. Again, it doesn't have to be a big change.

Running with a runner who is faster than you are is another good way of improving your speed. Suppose you average 15:45 for your local cross-country course. One of your teammates usually completes the course in 15:25. Try running the course, stride for stride, with your teammate. To keep up, you may have to increase the length of your stride or move your legs faster—or both.

Anytime you're seeking to improve, you should check your form for flaws. Any one of the faults listed below can serve to cut your speed.

• Poor posture—Letting the upper body tilt forward causes a shift in your center of gravity. That can lead to a shorter stride. The solution: Run tall.

Some runners allow their heads to fall forward when fatigue sets in. This also causes your center of gravity to shift forward, distorting your stride. Always keep your chin up.

• Improper arm action—When the arms pump, the hands should go forward and back. What you shouldn't do is allow the arms to pump from side to side so that the hands cross in front of the chest. This causes you to run unbalanced and reduces your speed.

• Too much knee lift—This is wasted effort, leading to fatigue, a lower rate of leg movement, and, ultimately, a loss of speed.

• Fingers tightly clenched—If you're guilty of

Be sure your arms pump forward and back, that you're not bringing your hands across your chest.

this failing, there's also likely to be tenseness in your arms and upper body. Your forehead is probably deeply wrinkled and you're wearing a scowl. Relax; tension causes fatigue. The tips of your fingers should be just touching your palms.

• Bouncing—Shorter than normal strides and poor arm action can lead to an up-and-down movement. Be sure each of your strides serves to drive you forward.

Besides what you do in your regular training sessions, you can work on improving your form at one of the fifty or so summer camps that specialize in running. While some camps offer coaching and instruction in track and field, there are many others that specialize in distance running and cross-country.

Running camps cover a wide range. They offer terrain that varies from the flatlands of the Oklahoma prairie to the Rocky Mountain splendor where runners run at altitudes of a mile and more. Some coaches have only high school experience; others have coached Olympic runners. Costs also vary widely. Be sure to evaluate carefully the location, facilities, costs, number of staff members and the experience of each before you decide on a particular camp. All camps provide free brochures.

It's also important to choose a camp that suits your running ability. For instance, if you're used to averaging about 30 miles a week in your training sessions, don't pick out a camp where the athletes

run two or three times a day, logging 20 miles or more. Trying to fit into such a program will be a strain on you, both physically and emotionally.

You can find out about camps from advertisements in running magazines. Or ask your coach to recommend some to you.

The length of your stride, the rate of leg movement, and your posture are all technical factors having to do with running. There are also physiological factors. These have to do with the smooth functioning of your body and its parts, with your strength and flexibility.

60

The strength of your legs and upper body can have an important effect on how fast you run. The stronger you are, the faster you can move your legs and the longer your stride.

Strength training can help to make you run faster.

Your high school probably has a weight room or other facilities for strength training. Discuss a strength-training program with your coach. Once you embark on such a program, keep in mind that it is no substitute for the other types of training, for

The fun that comes from being part of a team is one of running's benefits.

interval work or distance work. Strength training should merely supplement your regular running program.

Improving your flexibility can also work to build your speed. With greater flexibility, you achieve a greater range of movement with your legs and arms. You can take bigger strides; you can pump your arms with more efficiency.

The basic muscle groups you want to work on are those of the legs, knees, ankles, hips, lower back, and shoulders. A number of exercises that will help to stretch these muscles are offered earlier in this book in the section titled "Warming Up." Your coach can recommend others.

Muscle flexibility also provides for other benefits besides an increased range of leg and arm movement. It helps to improve your coordination and aids in preventing sprains, strains, and other such minor injuries.

Finally, there are psychological factors that can help make for running improvement. You have to have a positive attitude toward your ability as a runner. You have to believe that you can improve and you have to have a deep-seated desire to want to do so. And you have to maintain that desire despite the stiffness, soreness, pain, and fatigue that every runner experiences.

It is not easy. But the fulfillment you get from being physically fit, being part of a team, competing, and winning can make all the barriers worth conquering.

GLOSSARY

ACHILLES TENDON—The tendon at the back of the heel that joins the calf muscles to the heel bone.

BELLY BREATHING—A system of breathing in which a person expands his or her belly on every inhale and flattens the belly when exhaling (and which is recommended for distance runners).

BOX IN—To block, surround, or hem in an opponent during a race, so as to force the rival to drop back or go wide to pass.

BUNCHING—A race tactic in which members of a team run together in a group.

CARDIOVASCULAR SYSTEM—The bodily system that includes the heart, lungs, and blood vessels.

CHUTE—The passages set up beyond the finish line of a large meet through which runners must pass so their exact order of finish can be recorded.

DUAL MEET—Competition between two cross-country teams.

FARTLEK—Swedish for "speed play," a type of training in which the runner alternates periods of hard running with light jogging.

FIELD—The total number of runners in a race.

FLATS—Lightweight training shoes without any spikes.

FOOTPLANT—In striding, the action of the foot being placed on the ground.

GLYCOGEN—The principal carbohydrate storage material and a major source of energy whenever the body puts forth intense effort.

HAMSTRINGS—The muscles at the back of the thigh and knee; also the tendons at the back, or hollow, of the knee.

HARRIER—A cross-country runner.

INTERVAL TRAINING—A system of training in which the runner alternately sprints and jogs over set distances.

INVITATIONAL MEET—A cross-country meet among invited teams.

KICK—A burst of speed near the end of the race that carries the runner across the finish line.

LSD—Abbreviation for long slow distance, a type of training run.

LONG-DISTANCE RACE—A race of a mile or more.

MATCHING—A racing tactic in which each member of a team is assigned to out-run a rival team member.

MIDDLE-DISTANCE RACE—A race of 440 yards (400 meters) or 880 yards (800 meters).

NATIONAL FEDERATION OF STATE HIGH SCHOOL ASSOCIATIONS—The governing body of cross-country running (and about thirty other sports) on a high school level in the United States.

PACE—A runner's rate of movement for a specific distance.

QUADRANGULAR MEET—A competition among four cross-country teams.

QUADRICEPS—The large muscle at the front of the thigh.

SPIKES—Low-cut, lightweight track shoes with nail-like projections fitted to the sole, or the sole and heel, and used for sure footing.

SPRINT—A race of up to 220 yards, or 200 meters.

STARTER—The official responsible for the start of a race. He directs the runners as they line up behind the starting line, fires the starting pistol, and calls false starts.

TAPE—The length of string or yarn stretched across the track several feet directly above the finish line that is used to aid the officials in determining the winner of a race.

TRIANGULAR MEET—Competition among three cross-country teams.